Also by Lucky:

These Things I Crave
Water Media
Violent Words for Beautiful People
Inside Dark Light

Contact: sakulryder@gmail.com

Portrait Photo by
Riel McGuire

Inside Dark Light
©2012 Lucky Ryder

ISBN 978-1-7774688-3-5

All rights reserved.

No part of this publication may be reproduced, distributed or transmitted in any form or by any means, electronic, mechanical, photocopying, recording or otherwise, without the prior written permission of the author.

# O.G. INDIGO
## Lucky Ryder

CONTENTS

| | |
|---|---|
| 09 | BLOOD ON MY SHOES |
| 13 | STAIN |
| 14 | SYMPATHETIC OPHTHALMIA |
| 16 | CRESCENT SUNS |
| 19 | RESCUE |
| 23 | THE FAULTS OF PEACE AND SAFETY |
| 27 | TONGUES IN THE STOMACH OF A WIND DOE |
| 31 | MOON SHINES AT NIGHT |
| 34 | GLASS SHATTERING UNDER WATER |
| 37 | ESCHER |
| 39 | THE DOLDRUMS |
| 44 | LANTERN LIT PATHS |
| 45 | SPEAKERBOX |
| 46 | THE HUMAN CONDITION |
| 49 | THE COME DOWN |
| 52 | KOLI POSE |
| 57 | THE LAND BETWEEN SOLAR SYSTEMS |
| 60 | WHERE THE SWING LINGERS |
| 62 | A RECORD SLOWLY BACKSPINS |
| 63 | ICKERRBAK |
| 68 | STRAIGHT RAZOR SIGHS |
| 71 | CROCODILES |
| 74 | BRAND NEW T-SHIRTS |
| 75 | LABRADORITE |
| 76 | PROCESSING LIGHT |

| | |
|---|---|
| 77 | MIND YOUR MATTER |
| 78 | WHERE THE JEANS WEREN'T |
| 79 | FOR ROJIN'S GRANDMOTHER |
| 83 | LONGBOARDERS IN THE NIGHT |
| 86 | HARDENED SOFTLY RITUALS |
| 87 | A FIRE'S COMA |
| 90 | FLIP |
| 92 | JUSTICE |
| 95 | TWO BRIGHT STARS |
| 96 | YOU CAN'T SEE ME |
| 99 | HOWL ZEPPELIN |
| 103 | GRIMOIRE |
| 104 | FORGIVE |
| 105 | I ONLY WANT TO LIVE |
| 106 | BLUE |
| 107 | THE REED'S NOTE |
| 109 | AS I REACH MY REPLY |
| 111 | AURORA |
| 112 | DAFFODIL |
| 113 | PIRATES |
| 114 | A WHISKING EXISTENCE |
| 115 | REPLENISH |
| 118 | PAGAN |
| 119 | STANDING GROUND |
| 121 | PLAGUE APRON |
| 122 | 12 FOOT SPEAKER SPOKE THE LION NOW WATCH ME FLOAT |
| 123 | TOP HAT |

| | |
|---|---|
| 125 | RONIN |
| 127 | WHALE BONES |
| 130 | PERENNIAL |
| 131 | RUNNING FROM REAPER |
| 134 | GREEN TEA AND WEED SMOKE |
| 135 | UNDERWATER SONGS TO DIE TO |
| 137 | MAY YOUR TEA NEVER GO COLD |
| 139 | THE YARD |
| 140 | SAFFRON |
| 142 | OMNITEMPO MAXIMALISM |
| 143 | AND ON / NOD |
| 144 | NOD / AND ON |
| 145 | BOTTLED GODS |
| 147 | HEAD TILT EARTH CUBE |
| 148 | STILL MY SKULL'S SHADOW |
| 150 | DARK JADE TORTISE |

# BLOOD ON MY SHOES

I'm skulking around with blood on my shoes.
Got my neck in a noose with nothing to lose.
Soaking up sounds, the hood and the bruise.
Paths that I choose,
their elements brewed by alchemist crews.
I'm a rocket's caboose
cuz I guess the less hooch you use
you lose if not boozed.
I'm gaining moons
like daylight's coming too soon.
Slender shadows of the dunes
grow from midnight's bloom.
I cut right through
and make my own room to move.

And a lot of things are dousing these days.
Lord knows I do,

see the doom in the willow,
the womb of the killer,
the red eye fly by
tails light in the night sky
and I'm out here like a bad suture.
I'm busting out of this situation
on an early departure.
But I've had a lot of back slides

so now I'm skitching,
man, don't bother.

Park the car.
My harbored jaw
cracks like glass.
I evaporate with the solvents
into atmospheric toxins.
I've been tripping for so long
I'm only sober when I'm on it.
I don't know which way is up,
my mouth filling with water.
Don't know if it's raining or flooding
or maybe it's just in the air
like being in a sauna.

A frozen heart, now pardoned.
A lot of waste, no longer garbage.
A longer face I can no longer manage.
A tainted trace,
with grace I am vanished.

...

I've cried lakes into my palms.

Songs and psalms from hands that yawn
that bend with dawn and days be gone

and all that rum and smoke be done.
My kingdom come and bell be rung.
My queen from pawn
and rook to knight
to dead crown crawl
my presence, slight.

I pour and I storm and I make like lightning.
I mourn and I praise like a stray maze's ending.
I gaze and I haze in a constant amazement,
blessedly humbled by a moment's engagement.

Now I'm up, but I'm down,
with a brokenness in the water.
I'll float because I know how to sink.
I know my silence
because I know how to speak,
and I know at the peak
the air thins out.
It gets hard to breathe,
can't see for the clouds
can't hear for the shouts.
But with these two hands
I can feel for the routes
to the islands in the skies
I am fed by their roots.

I am bedded down on soft ground

and them branches be my roof.
The earth is still my skin.
See,
here I am,
the proof;

ending as I began
nothing more but nothing less.
A balance point of grace projected.
I need only to trust
in the honesty of my reflection.
Let my inflection bend my perception
so that I may see the inherent beauty
and perfection of all life.

Beginning with my own.

May I be given myself
so that I may give of myself.
Blessed be
and as always,
peace.

# STAIN

This sly cat slits under wide brimmed hats.
Soaked by grins since supplied
thine buckets of jack, gin, and rye.

Rusted cogs can fry the phat
chewed betwixt contingence,
and what was known as liquid composition.
Drafted in the grain cross marks
of the marble shrine.
Wanting jade light spit twice
skipping across the iris pool
of my bulimic third eye.
Sought where one could only derive.
Under these clothes
are the only rivers
where the rose hip lies.

No liquor? No sty.
No loose skull of symbiotes
too sober to fly.

Best fiddle to die
is the first spanning riddle
of this splitting mind.

## SYMPATHETIC OPHTHALMIA

Drifting off in a hot bath one night
my eyelids fall to the sound
of vocal samples and didgeridoos.
Drums in length
that peel me like lavender,
or a deep rem cycle.

I find myself in a water main
curving along my spine
underneath the occipital lobe.

The faucet drips as my toe slips.

The dripping is dark,
while the echoes are green.
The walls taste like rust
and cut my tongue to birthday ribbons.

How does anything exist
when nothing can be seen?

I walk the length of the water main.

Dangle my feet at the drop off.
The echoes are now hues of blue,

and then nothing.

If there were a piano here
I would play it.

Over the years my eyes reach the size
of my skinny swinging fists.

The silence has become
more than I can hear,
less than I can touch,
nothing I can see.

...

I just want my girl.

## CRESCENT SUNS

On late at last on summer nights
when the dry voices taunt the grass to breeze.
With the singing voices of the children's mothers
I grasp from the branches of uprooted trees.
Oil-soaked feathers and tangled nets.
Forest fires I only set to leave.
I have never witnessed, never noticed,
the burnt earth beneath the stormy weather.
I've too many terms I've yet to set.
Too many words I will never be.

So many paragraphs I have never scribed,
I've seen this through but never seen it free.
I'll scrawl twelve drafts upon the window sill.
A dozen revisions of my epitaph.
I've got days on end and years to kill
and in their wake, I will take the stand,
take the floor, build a nest, have a seat.
Never conscious of the waning past
the candles flicker in the curving hallways.
They dim against my bending knees.

A prayer for the walls
against every closing door.
An attempt to enter,

each calling knock.
A prayer for the loss I've suffered,
under every gain more than I once thought.

A prayer for the wolves,
their licking teeth and pointing fingers.
Bent over my shoulder I never noticed,
the guilty one I am always figured.

A prayer for the cost
of what it took to realize.
Eyes fixed upon the horizon,
shining stars and setting nights.
Contemplating the colors in my head
I missed the orb burning bright.
Merry-go-rounds and paper pinwheels,
I've been too blind to see the rise.

Sometimes, under the curvature of crescent suns
there is just too much smoke and speed to see.
Sometimes, over the half way moons
there's just too much fucking smoke to breathe.

Crescent suns, their half way shape.
Promises I dreamt I meant to make.
The half way shape of crescent suns,
what is done, is done and done piss poor.
I've been too concerned with what is more.

What is sore is what is left for me to take
and when what's done is gone.
When the moon is here,
when the sun has shone,
you'll find me in the forest fires.
A hanging scarecrow.
A fucking fake.
You'll find me nothing more
than the space between the horizons.
A half way man.
A half way shape.
Nothing left but what the sky can take.

# RESCUE

But the sky scrapers skinned us into a hole of hard earth.
Exasperated and tired out. A trusted pendulum swinging
heavy. A shining star scaling the blanket it clings to,
wide then gaping.

Against the grandfather clock the nine planets aligned.
Brandished behind the sweating sun setting transient
in a long line of what used to be the time,
we wouldn't consume.

Well now the skyscrapers may have us skinned at first light,
under the pungent afternoon of waking to the still scent of
draping locks of lavender lapsing towards our palms. The
tunnels we dug in the hills keep our glowing mosses warm.
Ambient under the darkened bodies of deciduous
and coniferous. A descending place to sleep,
calm and steady, for years to come,
for days on end if that's what's meant for us.

Waxing and waning, deep
inside this heavy mellow earth.
Substantial and brooding.
Smoldering coals,
camp fires litter the banks.
River fires visible from space
and music that connects us.

Resounding through the halls. Hills for homes. Heaven's shaking stalks quaking at the sounds. Columns slim and ascending. Waves of rain and light cascading. Directions converging on the swelling life, the light's depending.

Now what animal will I be when I'm the one
with heart strings and conscious lines connecting?
A vessel on all fours my heart is sore from the pounding.
Break beat chambers within me are a map to my
surroundings. A muzzle muttering for more softly
in his sleep, can you see my breath on the floor?

Filling footprints
sparking toenail filaments
traipse over the threshold
set against the bottom of the door.
These are the paths I set for myself in remembrance.
Paths I knew that I would one day need again
to follow four footed and vicious.

Calm and steady, a glass sphere on fingertips.
A warming earth, eggshell fragile.

A whisking existence treading so lightly.
Shovel wide teeth grinning shameless.
A universal scream to behold.
Barks that bite at the sky and chew through you.

Hair and bone.
Endless valleys of chest and stomach,
shadows scathed in waiting.
A bleeding, weightless bite to reconcile.
A continuum of you, star eyed and powerful.

Now what I mean to say is what I mean to be, that there is star power in your eyes. A depth that reflects the Saturn ringlets of both timeless and endless. Open as the atmosphere, controlled chaos swimming wise among the silence. Past the vanishing point of perception. Through what we think we know of the tangible world around us. Eons away from what our elders preached about redemption. All the supposed salvation we once accepted simply because it was an answer to all those questions.

Now know that behind our eye's reflection is more than just a window, but a veritable silo. Busting, concerning something more, something deeper than earthly religion with all of its deteriorating connotations. Something that shoots through my veins, riddles me to the core. Shakes and detonates my bones, an inner quake that I am begging for.

Now what animal will I be when I'm the one
with heart strings and conscious lines connecting?
A vessel on all fours my heart is sore from the pounding.
My eyes are tearing, bleeding, exasperating.

I have found love under the skin
that the sky has torn and stripped me of.

High above my soft scalp
I have found answers in the atmosphere,
and with every breath I take and every step I make
I am learning of my already present salvation.
It is out there.
Far beyond the mountain peaks
and past where the clouds
can no longer be seen behind me.

It is here behind my iris, behind my eyes.
Photographs of it are caught in the tears
that run down my cheeks,
drip onto my arms and sides.
I can hear the vibrato
echoing in the chambers
against my heart strings,
and we cannot smell,
or hear, or taste, or see.

But I am touching the connection.
It is warm and it is breathing.
A glowing reflection

I am rescued.

# THE FAULTS OF PEACE AND SAFETY

Under the willow tree I sit and wonder,
how the shaking limbs of an instrument
can make our hearts to fall.

And how the number of leaves
upon the dying life of this broad tree,
will only lessen in the shadowed spaces
over growing the grasses
of where we once grew tall.

Of what we will become
once we are no longer dredged
in a false sense of peace and safety,
set upon us by those dredged in a false sense
that we were at one point left unprotected and afraid.

Of what we will grow into;
our faiths, our disbeliefs,
our sudden realizations,
our aspirations caustic as waterfalls.

Contemplating what words we hear when
the violins overcome the static under the radio.
Bleeding out from the edges of our refrigerators.

What will we be when our sustenance dries out,

dries up towards the shrinking roots?
Will the apples fall farther from our tongues
than once predicted by our predecessors,
and will the will and whims of impulse
slow to stagnant palpitations?

The hand grasps quill across parchment
to scrawl out what we thought we meant.
That perhaps all of it may not all just go to waste.

Destroyed.

Empty as the heart compartments
cut into our gasping, dusted chests.
Withered as the cysts
upon the skeleton lips
of our dead and dying gods.

The flimsy matchbooks
under our lapels,
bursting at the seams;
fractured and flaming.
There will come a deadly wave
that will leave us with nothing.

So as I speak, so the words dissipate.
And as I love still, still my blood will stand still.
And the spirits of all life on earth are expendable.

But just as the broken chords
may sing loudly,
cannot help but one day
sing a little less than yesterday.

Cassette tapes disintegrate.
Brittle bones may fornicate.
Tearing heads and limbs
may scream out to another.
Clawing, scratching to communicate.

And the light gracing our scalps will fade.

There is no hope, but that which we create.

There are few things that I know,
and fewer things that I know to be true.
But one of those things is that my soul
is as full as it is desolate,
and yet even at this very moment
the light runs deep through my head,
with love and a reason to be passionate.
And even in the static and death,
and the running shaking cold.
The hate curling around the earth,
grasping taking hold.

That light sings to me from the hilltops
and I will on concave heavens stand,
and let hate know that it shall not pass.

And when my voice fades and cracks away,
and smokes away from the radio waves.
Look and know and see that I will always be,
everything that I need to be.
Look and know and see, I gained it all,
the day life's waves washed over me.

# TONGUES IN THE STOMACH OF A WIND DOE

A hawk child enamored.
Alone so suddenly.
'You are now free to scour'
harkened the dove mother.

You know that I've been waiting for you
to drop me from the branches for some time now.
For weeks, I've been speaking of it in my sleep.

Remember when we used to dream each other's dreams?

When I shook from the apnea,
and you whispered soft blue winds
to calm the veins of the leaves in my mind,
that tugged my spastic muscles into
fearful frets that could not stand the test
of your fingertips across my bald head.
The soft 'settle, shh it's ok, it's ok, settle.'
Dripping into my ears until the willow branches
graced the dirt leaving me calm and steady,
and sleeping sound once again.

Remember how we seemed to float in those days?

Remember how we just, fucking, floated?

We were birds and spirits and jet aeroplanes.
Waterfalls and free falls,
birds gliding on fire, doused in flames.

We were all the things
that never touch the ground.
A perfect silence under tilting wings.
Moving together, never a sound.

Stronger than cornerstones,
more resilient than cobblestone.
We were the wind and the clouds,
and the rain and lightning that fell from them.

We were a four lunged entity separated at birth
and every time we made love was a tireless effort
at linking rib cages and sewing hearts.
Mouths and throats that twisted between
jaw and spine to find perfect new homes
in each other's palpitating, craving bodies.

Palms to palms and bones to bones.
Finger tips pressed into joined ellipses.
Falling into the cracks of you because
those were the spaces left for me to fall into.

Remember how we seemed to shine in those days?
Remember how we just fucking shined?

Perfect setting horizons
cradle the rising stars in night,
casting shifting silhouettes
of us against the sky.

Two spirits clashing
      then residing.
A storming subtle wind I am
destined to ride the tides of.

I know that you've been waiting
for me to drop you from the branches
for some time now. For weeks,
you've been speaking of it in your sleep,
and I fear if we do not fall now
we will never again fly free.
Frozen in the snow
above the rutting of the wind does.
We would surely cease the blood in one another.
Never taste the west or southern shores and sea.

For as perfect as we may have been
in amongst the leaves of the trees
we built for ourselves; we will always
fall through the cracks in one another.
For those spaces have now become
too wide for each other to cover.

The tides are rising
and the weather is changing.
It is time that we shed
these tired and weary feathers
and reveal the true colors
of a dividing flight path.
The last of migrations
and long journeys
that we will make together.

Birds do not fly backwards
over the hooves of the wind does.
For this has never been,
nor will ever be
the way the grass blows.

## MOON SHINES AT NIGHT

A midnight summer rain fills the small space between rooftops. Tugging the wafting traffic lights into arching gradients that pull their shifting pixels onto the cobblestone below.

Rested against the brick wall with my knees to my chin in Fan Tan Alley. Teardrops of light glimmer radiantly between the studs of my belt and the patches along the bottom of my black hoodie, where peeks a pair of soft pink panties.

The aroma of oysters and rack of lamb drift from an open kitchen door. A plank of light cuts across against the back of my hand where I breed shadowy puppets upon darkened window panes. Heavy, as the gray smoke that collects in my hood, skewing the nuance of glow across my face lifting from the cherry that spirals about on point of a stout black cigar. The object of my current absent-minded vanity and affection.

You are a mother as the Moon shines at night.

Though we have only just met
you teach me that safe places
do not only exist outside of
the rain and foul weather.

You are a mother as seeds bend towards light.

Though we have only just met you teach me
that sometimes, dry lands crack and bleed the skin.
That floods are necessary to float together the pieces
meant to build a wet and safer kind of shelter.

When you return from the restaurant washroom you reach into your left breast pocket, retrieve a small white box and offer me another cigar. These are a warm chocolate brown. Long, slender, and remind me of old Burmese women and board games I've never played. You comment on the black and white photography, the sheen of the steel faucets and a religious tract you glanced at in the top of the waste basket.

In your absence I will dream of lips against the reed of a woodwind. Eyes of storms where the palm trees are steady. Places inside myself where there is no such thing as sin and the shelters you taught me to build in the dry heat of chaos, they will be the strongest, because I know that there is a time for war and when that day comes, I will be victorious, for I am learned and ready.

When I close my eyes,
you are standing alongside the ocean's surface
swathed in white linen absorbing the moon light
that falls only upon the few beautiful women
I feel fine enough to call mother.

The space above your head
is constantly swarming with doves
white as light from which all color we stole.
In my absence, please remember
that it is the heart of the black birds
that are waiting for you
to fill them with your soul.

## GLASS SHATTERING UNDER WATER

Thoughts that talk are thoughts once sought,
and talking thoughts are songs that are taut.
Between the spheres we toss from jelly and starfish
unto organic stillness as living as the moss
embodies a moment is precious,
on all levels of existence.

From the sloth in the tree tops, to the oceans deep
where I become lost in the belly of darkness,
accented by microscopic luminescent life
as conscious as they are asleep all around me.

Maintaining density at a depth
I've never been submerged to before.
The echoes of anemones,
soft glow of organic phosphorescence
the stillness, it speaks to me,
and in turn I am singing.

Your attitude and presence comfort me
to temperate degrees of which I cannot imagine.
Upon engaging, more so than I could
have ever contrived (even in poetry).
Your tendrils and transparencies
seemingly never complete.
Breathe like with the breaking waves

that you've never seen.
In such silence I swear the sound
of the electricity in my body
is that of you singing to me.
Still in subtle turn I am speaking
in scattered separate tones.
An influx of pressure parts for the song.
It is of the closest distance
the way my voice is through the phone.
The way I am shattering under water.
Cradled by the curve of lacing coasts.
Coaxing the height of high rises
heavy beneath the surface currents.

Glass spheres shifting, swiftly sinking,
waiting to be swallowed wholly
in by the slinking anemones.
The whales tender throats,
by the vibrato of all remnants
of the bottom of the ocean floor
to the roofs of skies and seas.
There are atmospheres,
beneath my feet.
Knees swept softly against
the inner harbor, outer bay.
What is that you sing to me?
Sounds which alone convey
cracks in the earth's core

rotate the deep ocean waves.
My transparency is unbinding
as the phosphorescence behaves.
To bare light inside the fractured splinters
of so many glass spheres shattering under water.

Up turned geometries.
Angles and pressure gauges
of which I am not concerned.
Air tanks I know,
that I do not deserve.

But without the light I cannot see
where I begin or where I end,
so I am as endless as I allow myself to be.

Completely stripped of all reserve.
These fragments are a reminder
of the omnipresence of a moment.
Every skipped beat,
is every silence I hope with.

## ESCHER

A brick falls
from the apex of the ceiling.
Your head detained, accepts a dull thud.
Derailed enroute to radio static smacking.
Oil paints across pale cheeks raise the color.

Floored sculptures like you
are art for the blind.

Braille bound
upon hardwood contingence.
Conveyer belts that drift you
from winded soul into
the space between wet walls
with every out stretched hand.
Only farther still, away from me.

Dark spots fade to closed eye visuals.
Embossed and delaying sumi-e ink
runs these golden limbs
rush
down the spiral staircase.
Cement tiles twist
flicker in a flash.
A rain of things betwixt this scientist
breaks the sky beams into focused light

which pulls at my heart strings,
ashed as thumbed hash screens
describes the diagnosis.

The lamps that lit my progress
are destined to set the hay ablaze.
Visible from the widest points
of the paths I made.
To embers glow against our bones.

A single hair between my lips,

you are prostrate
and already dead.

I was just trying to build you a home.

# THE DOLDRUMS

I must admit that I could never remember the days when the slayings were intentional. Regardless of the many moons we stood under upon stone monuments that rose from the so few mounds we carved in droves and circles. This ashen esophagus of mine has cried just the same every day since the rain came in flocks of pillars within that Trojan paper crane. I recognized my waning, only as affection waxed in pale star light between an anvil and the hammer of a soul's crescent temple. Perhaps if the smoldering coals were objects capable of reflection the palms of your hands and fingerprints may have been something more familiar to me. Maybe even the midnight dousing would have been some kind of sanctity promising anything I could have contrived, at least as longevity. Pooling in your cupped hands. Slowly tiding between the metaphysical cracks and kindling. A haughty glance from the corner of our twin born eyes purple and skewed amidst the heavy laughing.

I know.

I know if I breathe the dust just deep enough I can still black out to soliloquies we penned together on the back side of beautifully vulgar Polaroids of you, spread eagle and bottom lip biting. Destitute, mellow and brooding are the angels drenched in composites that visit me now and again when the lights go out and I find my skull's arrestment between the dirt and the floorboards, the heaving contractions and the doldrums.

Beings as separate and emotional
as they speak directly and individual.
Life forms exist in as much as what
we know to be sound, as in as what
we trust to be based in carbon
(I learned that from you).

I must admit that what I remember the most is that day behind the emerald drapes when you taught me how to eat the children of the songs we sang into existence. The sustenance, was more than overwhelming. The abundance was sure to go to waste. I never told you this but I was never capable of coping. The density and breadth of what I was growing exponentially to know as love, was a landscape so vast I was scared into hiding. For fear that my digital and canvas renderings would be projected as imperfect deliveries to an audience of jeering Emily Carr graduates. Bison eyed and jaws, elephant tusked and wide for the killing fields from days of street car grappling long since passed. New York, Chicago, Detroit; cocksuckers that brandished sabers spelt in the east coast snow. The way deceptive leering shackled attic studio movie making into fits of rage turned acid blotter snuff film endeavors. Those memories seemingly so independent of one another. But these are the subtleties that connect the left and the north to the right and the south

hemisphere. Calgary. Black Rock City. Victoria. These were the bone yards where I built beseeched and cobblestoned bomb shelters, I knew for textbook certain to be capable of meeting the dose. Stemming inside from underground, where the blackness was complete.
Where I knew it would hurt the least,
and the most.

I led you in by a fingerless hand, traced the hallucinations across your technicolor eyelids, and without a sense of touch or sight, taught you the lip-reading palette of awakened stone ghost hosts I had chipped from the space between knuckles, to gain the wisdom of forgotten widths of the color wheel planks. Having painted two new irises onto your body I assumed once you had learnt my wanting language you would be better able to see with. Walk, stalk, hunt and make the necessary kill with. Open up the throat of your captors, the graduates. Come back home to me once and for all. Fuck, flame, and destroy that sinking left behind nothingness of a slave ship.

But the doldrums were a rocketing downward anchor that pierced your side by surprise. Drug you down to the oceans deep from where sincerely sinful and plotting monsters are derived. It was there in the crushing cradle of your own rut and defeat, you yourself learned the powerful lesson of what it is like to never awaken from a dream.

While through symbiotic karma I was thrown pieces of the nightmare that came at me in fragments. A true captive of your entanglement I am pried from the safety of the bomb shelter's basement. The tongue cut from my mouth as I tried to give way to your testament. Buried to the neck and left for dead alongside the rising tides disengaging embankment.

While through it all, I whispered last words and prayers I could have never possibly spoke. But if I had a joint in hand or an arm to raise it, I'd dedicate the smoke to you and the burning weed to me. Kiss the cherry and take one last toke, for all the hauls I believed meant the most. A tear from my right eye would land on the sand and in it's reflection all of the true lies we spilt on one another and never seemed to give a damn. Refractions of everything I'll ever be, and everything I already am. Reflections of the wisping smoke as it rose to the sky, and I must admit that what hurt the most as my mind went black, as I felt myself die.

It's that you weren't there beside me,
your shuttering eyes staring back into mine.
And if there was one thing
that I could say in this moment
I would scream for all that is holy,
and all that is right,
that every second spent without you
I was fucking electronic on the inside.

For a life lived as a gadget harbors no happiness.
At least none that I could find.
A life lived as scrap metal rusting
away into fragments is a life lived
simply waiting for the power
in the double As to subside.

So, for all that it's worth
and all of the nutrients in the dirt
found under the grass upon earth.
Peace out for now, to whom it may concern.
I know I'll see you on the other side,
where the only ocean we swim in
is an ocean we know as love and pure light.

## LANTERN LIT PATHS

In a forest full of stages,
it's always brighter where the music is.

## SPEAKERBOX

I did it.
I finally fucking did it.
I've overdosed on music
and I'm an angel now
floating just above my body.
I can see myself sitting there.

You can look in the forest.
You can search in the streets.
You can check in the club
but sure as hell
you won't find me.

Dumbed out on acid, propped
up against a 7-foot speaker
with 90,000 watts of sound
blasting out around my body.

You can look in the forest.
You can search in the streets.
You can check in the club
but sure as hell
you'll never find me.

## THE HUMAN CONDITION

At the sound of these chimes
I find my rhymes persistent.
Propagating positive lines
like I'm getting a fine dime
for every time a mind's been lit with
the light of my tongue's a diamond.
Perfect sides that reflect consistence.
Mirror images bend to ways of that of my mystics.
Transcend synonyms of my soul
that I don't know like secrets.

That's why I tend to my family.
Our castle and moat. The throne is our own,
cuz they the surrounding spirits
that know where the lungs and home is
and when one of the tribe is fucked with
we armor clad battle honed and steady.
Slithering out of Rome,
got a handful of gonads at our right hands.
Our cronies grin's glimmering
behind helmets shimmering.
Appendages fingering towards the hilts
of swords we forged from serpents.
Built with love, and that's why we shove relentlessly.
Endlessly our wrists are framed by white cuffs.
Sharp as a surgeon stuffed with Ritalin,

urging for a patient.
A skin ticket, a slit in the right divot
a twist on the spout of the right spigot.
Curve the words, extinguish the hate,
relinquish the state of the sounds we made.
Hammer and sickle and socket and spade.
Laid from the dirt into mounds.
Reconditioning the ground
we may reposition landscapes,
but what of the heartscapes
and what do the storms say?

Do tell. What are the depths
of this furious well that flourishes well?
What are the composites of the human condition?
What are its systems?
Where is the book of shadows to its spells?
Here's a paper and pencil, write that down and list them in order of where they're bound from, where they are going and where I can catch them. Because I got inside information that recognition of these human traits as weaknesses is dangerous. Because I'm experiencing symptoms deemed slanderous. And we're coming to grips with our old sickly position. Maybe bone thin still thickly spun hazardous. Waste contaminates our taste.
The similarities amidst our breathy kiss
betwixt the mist, we trace the lips of our brethren.
Hope spattered, community laced, racing the endorphins.

It's like were all dreaming the same dream.
So take me to a place
unlike anything I've ever seen.
Unlike anywhere I've ever been.
Where the only machines propagate beauty
and a sound that is near haunting.
Sound that fulfills and never leaves me wanting.
Where we're never walking
we just glide on the tones
like we're practically floating.
So take me to a place
unlike anything I've ever seen,
unlike anywhere I've ever been.
A place inside,
where we know what we can be,
where we know what can be reached.
So take me.

# THE COME DOWN

The table tops are sloppy.
Ashtrays overflow,
chair legs unscrewed, wobbly.
The whiskey spilled this time
what I'd call too far away from my body.
No longer joint custody,
still held responsible,
wrongly.

My mind's grown far too bawdy
feeling so alone in somebody else's home
jumping with so many bodies.
These limbs are not my own.
These lips cannot, I cannot own.
Too raw, too tawdry.
No love between them, tasting far too salty.
Walls are breathing and spinning
like I'm in the laundry
and I wonder why I can see my ghost
spryly, smiling beside me.

So I be faint like a crook
and steal away slowly,
to that of my dose, my hook,
take it in wholly.
Thanks for the bump,

appreciated homie.
Thanks for the cap,
but I'm already rolling.

All kinds of shit stirring inside
and moving on through me.
Whoa, I'm coming up way too fast.
I'm kind of losing control.
Wait, what did you say?
I can't seem to understand you.
Oh god, I think I copped too much
I can't even stand up.
Better grasp onto the banister.
I know it was too much,
don't tell me I told you.

Only six more hours 'til the come down.
Just going to have to wait this shit out.
But fuck I'm tripping balls.
Just prop me up against the wall,
hand me my smokes and a lighter,
get me a lemon to suck on,
get me some water,
kill all the music and
turn all the lights on.

I'm sorry, but I do not know my location.
I am living and afraid of every thought

I am thinking. Falling apart one piece at a time
with every shallow breath that I'm taking.

Just a few more hours 'til the come down.
I know that I can make it.
I know I won't swallow my tongue
cuz I can taste the damage.
I know my brain is bleeding
but I don't know if I can manage.
Cuz right now I got the consciousness of a goldfish
and as far as I can tell, I've spent my entire life
in a birdcage, locked away and banished.

In retrospect I can tell you that the drugs work.
No doubt about it and I'm not trying to fill no hole.
Just trying to expand my horizons and feel more whole.

But sometimes in retrospect,
long after the come down.
I can tell you that the drugs,
they fucking work.
Sometimes almost too well.

## KOLI POSE

And you say you ain't got much left
save for the short end of a dime bag.
And I can tell by the way you're scratching at it
that you want that shit just as badly as I do.
But the reasons why we're both eyeing
that little baggie I know ain't the same.

You just want something to let you feel again.
Maybe this time, let you feel the pain.
Cuz yea it may hurt,
but at least that's something.

For too long I've been swimming
in this hint of tea and green and nicotine.
Sure, I could get a hit from the little ripsters
but could you hear me scream?
Especially with my .45,
what, am I willing to die?
Bullshit.

I've been scuffling a lot with these mean mugs.
Griping a lot about them tough drugs.
I been gripping a bottle of colt 45
so tight you best believe there's no slugs.
Pass on the rum but hand me the ganj'.
Hitting the bong, staying mentally strong.

The days are long, we're up 'til dawn
fronting like nothing's wrong,
but still, I just can't seem to get my fill
that image in my mind's eye sighs the same still.

Well I do what I can and I do what I will,
But my wanting wants more than I'm willing to kill for.
So I cut chems, rearrange brain stems,
advocate all kinds of trends and burn blends.

While all along there's been too many cigarettes,
and not nearly enough om steez. Jesus Christ,
what'll happen to the righteous might
when the strong leaves.

I scraped the grill so I could get my fill
on some of that burnt cheese.
Gel caps preferred.
(Pressed pills? You know I don't do that shit.)

But if you hold those sheets straight, please,
I'll breeze off the bend in the bee's knees
cuz when the streets bleed
I see only thin bones and long sleeves.
Sprocket pockets misunderstood,
so we understand how to mock drop
these midi keys. Sung seeds for trees.
Introduce liquid LSD into the sockets

of the botched rockets blasted fourfold for thee.
Keep the lips loose, and ass tight as the industries
cuz inside this piece I keep my Glock
assembled and stocked. Free of the trembles,
hammer cocked on my peace.

The chrome gleams in time
with the blood on the screen.
So much so, that you can't see me.
Residual quality you know me
and the product I sling.
But sight's going cost us
so the blindfolds are free.

Before the trail goes cold,
before the water goes deep.
Don't go still as green tea.
Grenades that don't sleep.
They only bide their time
under assumptions and alibis.
A learning curve,
steep roll of the tongue
like soft meat off the mind's eye.
Unlearn. Instigate. Identify.
Engage. Strengthen. Exhume. Confide.
Say baby, at least I got one thing right.

Decide if that's your style. If the hues are too lewd.

Construed notions butterflying planet earth's mysteries
and curses under the surface of the ocean's currents.
What's all this commotion spread like wildfire?
Razor sharp lotion. Sped spike mild flower.
How many soils can sour when in the case
of an hour, moons full you know devours.
Leaving nothing but a crow's aching skeleton
in the reflection of the pavement.
Empty spaces where windows once took refuge
in the top halves of towers. Glass trap doors
under the foundation of the basement.
Trawling the deep blue like icebergs
determined to melt off isolation.
Remains only a slip in the stacked clip.
A chip of a percentile.
Blown gaskets and castle roof tiles.
Merlin not noticed minor cracked rackets
or crimped hinges. Faults in positions,
the bending of what's with us.
Spells subjugated upon our enemies
blown to cigarette ash over time
eroded in a likeness to
the cancer face of their children.
There are no grimacing cringes.
Only blind eyes like Medusa cries.
No silver shields.
Helmets pulled back too high to hide.

If this is the way that I'm going to go
I'll be a feast of a meal. A riot ravenous.
Too staccato for corruption to conceal us.
No walls can contain us.

Dropping feet in the tide's fine sand.
Coordination hammered
as fork tines in Shiko stance.
Lancing lattices like lemurs and rabbits.
We can take this assault and grace it.

Folded steel splits where thick fog
spit light shines convinced.
Nine lives folded themselves like steam.
Not a single cry,
just a rush of the wall of sound.
Linger weightless before the ground.
Calm before the storm.
A faint crook in the trees.
A soldier on his knees.
Nothing left but these here three.
A single samurai survives.
Civilizations are born of a mind that can thrive.

# THE LAND BETWEEN SOLAR SYSTEMS

I take time to reappraise my new scars under an old sun.
Adaptations lending lies and truth to you
about who I am and where I'm from.
Constantly changing as it is consistently the same.
A grey haze atmosphere atop a cascading maze.
Psychedelia.
Green tea lights in the purple night.
The howls of mahogany wolves spilling
into the shadows of the footprints we made.
The fingertips across hips we traced.
Lips that solar flared with such self-similarity
to the universe they embodied,
I envisioned the heat intensely,
still wanting.
But the color burn is slow.
So slow that when it rolls it pulls on me, heavy.
I was covered in third degree from neck to toe, holy.

Traipsing the space of grass fires laid to light the way.
My position may have changed but it's still the same inside
my brain, in my lungs, between my nerves, under my skin.
The evolution is ambient so I keep tabs on the state that
my vessel is in and I take time to reappraise the similarities
between my sweat and the dew. Adaptations about who I am
and where I'm from lent lies and truth to you.

We will never gather all that we need to know about one
another until we can banish all time but the moment.
When we can come together as immediate humans creating
immediate experiences under visual atmospheres. When our
lovers can become our friends, and our friends can become
our lovers. When we can embrace one another as partners
conscious in that we can create a community based upon
ethical and social values. That pushes us to discover how few
barriers remain between what keeps us on the ground,
and what allows us to hover. Where there are no walls,
just waterfalls of movement. Niagaras of beauty and virtue.
An understanding of the necessity of unified concrescence.
Advanced appendages fingering the nexus with a sense
of wisdom and raw love harboring duty.

So I keep tabs on what it means to be a student.
What labs prove on the subject of universal influence.
Upon the internal thoughts, individual and fluid.
The artistry of mathematics born from superfluous
congruence. The breadth of it all often is portrayed as
confusing. But there's nothing wrong in the confusion.
All I know is the hurt, and not the source of my contusions.
So I do my best to stay wide eyed as a student. But still even
in the rain and the running, the hurricanes and the pain
and the study. I am not finding what I am looking for.

And so I take time to reappraise
my new scars under an old sun.

Find myself fascinated
by the land between solar systems.
The relationship between
the stones and the throwers,
the recipients and the victims.
I be the one with a rock in my hand
and a hole in my head.
I am not finding
what I am looking for,
and even if I did,
the questions would remain eternal.
So I don't stress the quests.
I stay well dressed and hope for the best.
Keep the snot off my shoes
and shoot for the moon,
cuz it's all in the fucking sky.
We're doing fine,
we're almost there.
Second star to the right,
and straight on 'til morning.

## WHERE THE SWING LINGERS

I write poetry to satisfy my oral fixation.
My hope for another generation.
My approximate detonation of ready triggers
sanctioned to be the bringer downers
I have bannered the final obliteration.

At which I scoff, and ask what for?
What of the toxic omissions
missioned from a darker place inside of me?
A carbon fission heart and a set of lungs
even with the energy of cold fusion,
spat on me and refused to start.

So what of my practices?
What of my spirituals, my rituals?
So what of my part? I was once asked
"What is it that we do art for?"

So I will ask myself again, why did you start?
Why did you take any part?
What is the purpose and why is your art?

I was once told,
"Once we get into the swing of things,
then we can start swinging things."

And I always wondered where it was that we had to go to find where the swing lingers. And how once we got there the swing would reconceive us into a womb that pulled us into a place that I don't remember. But I'm certain I had been there before without ever having had noticed until now with strained eyes sore.

The profundity
sometimes belittles me.
In that when I acknowledge
that I had been there before.
I am akin to realize
that I had never left.

I, had never left.

## A RECORD SLOWLY BACKSPINS

My toes between the sand.
The forest fogs wrap around my hand.
My heart under the needle,
endlessly tracing grooves within the vinyl.

The shivering breaks
induced by the flow my knees make.
Collapse this jaundice babe
and rise the nodding head
of the man that I have grown to be.

Of the spirit that I have made.
Of the tracks I have played.
Subliminal curses
hinting words in verses
on where I will come to lay.

Two records fade,
as one,
slowly,
backspins.

# ICKERRBAK

The dart sled roses grew in dusted fire
bended beneath the forest floor
at the foot of that great orchard.
Inside the softened sphere of lighting
the flames took their cause swiftly,
crackling in posture spoke relation.
Brethren of our waving hands and rising cheeks
sinching redder with the overture of another apple heart.
Sopping seeds and stars we carved.
A steel blade runs the length of thumbs to a nail,
string known and hips informed.

If only these were mine.
If only I was yours to own
we might spend the stone and agitate
acoustically in languages that only you could know.
You taught the serpents symmetry, the snow.
Starving hares we parented,
barbwired through the throat.
Beat tread paths that danced like we do in the fire
out of necessity, or to turn our nerve ends outwardly.
We were oaks with upturned roots
that lead us leave wherever we may go,
and wherever the sky boats tow;
there we will follow into a night
crossed as canvas hatches.

The bridges of branches wet as staved matches,
light up our way and point us to day,
with windows that glow and gates open latches.
Torches, there. North star, bare.
Spade shaped noses turned upward.
Gingerly we follow.
For the wretches of clouds
reflect the trenches of sounds.
Glinting as the leper shard mouths
stitched in a lax style, bound.
Accustom to corn rows,
gold leaf textured as kief
and coarse as the wool of a hound.
The hides we bled ground south from the poles.
Cadavers under ice. Heart beats melt the sleet,
the sheets of still Polaroid snow.

Through a thin layer of frozen water uneven
with the skin's palpitations the hazel flecks
of an iris skew in ellipses reminiscent
of the seed of the apple of your dissected eye.
Cut widthways, we embodied the shape of stars to come.
On lesser days we were glancing blows and pot shots,
mistaking the slipping blade for the rising of the sun.
The symmetry of freezing rain evens out our pores
and we appear younger in the white out,
than we ever have before.

When our shadows spread long enough
to bend up, across, and over
the white wash picket fence.
When our shadows spread long enough
to bend up, across, and over
the yellow as squash aging dog with no chance.
When our shadows spread long enough,
to bend up, across, and over the worn through walls
and roof of the home we built. But whose life
over the last decade had been tested and spent.

It was there and, in these hours,
that we allowed our powdered forms
a seasonal step from threshold.
Up across the caking dust plains,
stretched between the whispers
we panned from goldmine to one
another at the bottom of warm baths.
Lips locked with a fever we would
cross from cushioned caves
and screen doors in a tone,
wavering as cellophane.

The traceless scar skims the hairline of your face.
Your eyes accept the dust like lakes.
The dry heat and particles freckled our skin in circles.
Boney chest to perspiring nape.

Shoulders that bronzed the summit sun
summoned our brooding mouths dictation
from tractor chakra to cow tongue cuticle
into yoga positions reminiscent
of kung-fu studied sideways.

The only difference is that on today,
conjoining the curvature of shadow,
our lips bent ocular in an awkward attempt
to rise in the heat of what's best for our souls.
For our nest to sew what is left
so that they, in later years,
in an hour not unlike todays,
can hold their swollen jaws high
and in contest with a smile at rest,
and stand a chance in light
of the shades judging stance
we cast on a mushroom patch,
that we had nicknamed Hollow.

For that was the orchard
where we learnt how to swallow
and give way to a freedom
our joints thirsted for on the dust plains.
A process of the combining of our marrow.

When we fed, it was always on
the notion of an animal's dying child.

We are so sorry for the pain we've caused you.
We just mistook those vestiges for bile.

We stood above the infants.
Barefooted on shallow graves
as we watched their bodies stave and swell.
Twitch infectiously as if they were
the tunnels and home ways of something
larger than the spaces that contained them.
As if they were less when visible.
Wanting to disappear,
so that it/me/you/we/us
could again be as we should.
So that together,
we could finally be whole.
And I know.
I now know.

There are some bodies that never let go of their soul.

## STRAIGHT RAZOR SIGHS

A horse mill's melody
exists in it's rotation.
Though without closing hours
coupled with motionlessness,
the animals that work it
can never harbor the energy
necessary to trod and play.

So be reminded that the neighs of
your mare still grinding at twilight
are not soul songs in the light of luna,
but collages of neglection
matted together by shoddy camps
deployed in hindsight.
Warming fires not lit until first light.

Feedbags left to spoil.
Bits and the jaws that held them,
you never took the time to learn needed
nothing but soft hands and a calming tone.
Rather you assumed rested easier in mouths
if soaked in good intentions and oil.

Your feet may be bare so that you will always know
the lay of the land more intimately than us blacksmiths,
used to pounding around in knob nail shoes.

But on the gradient of this hill, what you believed was
carrots and mead freely given was so obviously labor
that never had the chance to come from a place of love.

But even an animal who has an intimate relationship
with their blinders, knows what words of guidance
are worth when there are no fingers through
their mane when they lay down to die.

But you don't care for yourself.

And a human's trust is only as worthy
as their heart remains still which in
the heat of the dark and moment
is sporadic, unusual,
predated, and honestly,
not that often.

I keep no work animals or pets.
No will that I recognize as my own,
but a communal understanding of the difference
between productive solitude,
and the gaps left in the earth by straight razor sighs
swung from the ankles of trunks en route.
Scouring the lay of land for creatures to grasp,
coddle and smother leaving nothing of an excuse
but blood on the roots and a scoff in the wind,
saying 'at least I tried.'

Over grown and foreign foliage choke out the forest
and when there is nowhere left for the animals to hide.
They'll find refuge at front of the claw foot furnace
that warms my nape and ember scuffed pant legs.

My back to the light.
Hammer against the anvil.

There are no words here.
No intentions.
Just a steady beating heart.
A path to travel,
and a home in sight.

# CROCODILES

I had a cat tails slink for turn tables,
home brew and jamming with you,
the dope pro on the dobro
and a hankering for hashish stew.
You know,
just kicking it like we do.

But I walked in the door,
and to my chameleon chagrin
stood shoulders turned in,
a single eye protruded.
Mouth cracked and drooling
for where I had before seen beer bottles,
paint markers and strewn clothing
reminiscent of parties gone by
and clairvoyant of art to come.
I found now, only desolation.

You at the counter
with flour on your hands
and pasta sauce on your feet
from when the jar shattered
on the floor as you turned.
Startled by my entrance that
slit the sucking silence.

I felt a breeze of depression
rushing over my skin as I said
'hey' and removed my shoes.
Trying vainly not to notice that
though it really wasn't that bad
the house seemed filthier
than it ever had before.

The same wine bottles, wall hangings,
cardboard canvases and cold chamomiles,
coated with a grim cringing grime.
I swear,
I could see a sheen of sickness on everything.

I stood in the middle of the kitchen
thinking about any place else I could go.
Anywhere besides here, besides my home.
I would sit and read but I didn't want the
shit from the walls and pages getting on me.
I would switch on the turntables and spin,
but I feared the sound would disgrace
the present and disgusted silence.
That the music that moves
would not be welcomed in.
So I sat on edge of the ledge, smiled,
and tried to give you the love I could
without falling face down in the current of the Nile.

Under certain circumstances
crocodiles are not choosy eaters
and will pick a rotting corpse clean.
No movement is necessary to draw their attention.

You were a twitching coma drowning in the
poltergeist you didn't know how to tell to leave.

It was just you and me
and a room full of ghosts.
Frustration and loneliness.
An atmosphere that grieves.
Humidity and the harbinger.
It's one hundred degrees in here
but there might as well be snow.
Freezing time and space
and dragging a bitter roux over
the very things that made us feel the most.

## BRAND NEW T-SHIRTS

I am doing my best to be the change.

To cleanse myself of the poison and grime
but I am addicted to the things I hate.

And sometimes that battle inside,
it spills out.

It gets on others.
On their brand-new t-shirts
they're so proud to have now.
On their dirty old shoes
they're ashamed to have to wear.

And I know I'm wearing the stains
of other people's battles too.
I'm sure you notice the splash and spray
as I myself tend to do.

So once in a while I will ask
that you pardon the war I am.

I am doing the best I can,
to love us both
as honestly as I know how.

# LABRADORITE

I am taken a step back.
Wept onto my knees by the beauty around me.
Waves that awash in walls corrode
and I am left with what becomes me.

A factory. A vestry.
A negative space of what I understand.
The ghosts well they do still pertain
glint differently under the looking glass.
No more questions are asked
then there are tunnels through my hands.
I am broken up, pushed aside.
Vanquishments of the creation
and destruction of universes
that I cannot attempt to hide.
No more alive on my feet
than I am dead on the sand.

I am broken up,
pushed aside

by the beauty and my understanding
of its relationship to who I am.

## PROCESSING LIGHT

Like with chemical bathes risen in the dark room, grains
that have latent image sites will develop more rapidly.

So is the arrested revealing, amplification and feeding off
the parts of myself that I don't need any more.

With every completed processing,
exposed and developed documentation,

I am ejecting the bones of the carcass of the scavenge
pecked and pawed upon under the dust of
the desert and dying trees of my soul.

Pick the scabs off my heart that have taught me to scorn,
and every day purer, more bathed in sacred light
than the very day on which I was born.

## MIND YOUR MATTER

When the shades come down
that's when the fires go out

and you can't see me.

Hood up,
I steam through the streets
as quickly as I please.

The hot air surrounding.

A swift breeze across your nape,
you turn to look a second too late.

In the exposed corners
touched by day light,
sly cats become shadows.

## WHERE THE JEANS WEREN'T

We opened a door a piece
inside the same moment.

Crushing dry wall.
Knobs meet in the center.
Brass bends under flagrance.
Flown to the rafters.
Fuck it.
The dust sleeps.

We wore headphones blaring opposite beats.
Timbre not the opposition.
Wolves lapping at the backs of our teeth.

Mesh prints scatter the bottoms of our feet.
Horizontal, our pulses pass and we are the same.
Contrast outside, thunk!
The tones daft.

The back of my knees quiver.
I feel the muscles tighten in my ass.

The morning after we will invent the revolving door.

I just need you to break my heart.

## FOR ROJIN'S GRANDMOTHER

If I could speak of the east in tonal languages deserving, I would use the hyperbole of words such as veritable and haunting. Full-bodied, manifesto, and grandmotherly. Really any sounds conducive of the ancient minds bred of a windful theory in music, and the sands mountaining on the eyelids of faith remind me of the most far off places within myself. Dunes sliding, even with my back turned. Singing sitars, seldomly stagnant circumvent under earth, running rivers. Wet palms, closer when you are at my side.

In a desert drenched in mirage, it is always more quenching where the music is, and if there is one thing that the visual guidance of Sanskrit has taught me it's that god is in the flow of characters streaming together. Words become emotion become manifestation like it has been every single day since the rain's apocalypse subsided, patiently.

Your grandmother,
is a beautiful woman.

The next time you see her, hold her face in your hands. Look into her eyes and tell her that somewhere there is a skinny tattooed Canadian boy standing barefoot on the harbor, covered in paint, cigar clenched between teeth, bobbing gently to the beat. Tell her that even though he is that far away and even though you have no idea who he is. When you smile with subtle grey eyes of love and knowing and confidence and strength, uncertain certainty, hope, peace, wisdom and honor; he can feel you, and he loves you, truly.

The chimes intact tinker heart songs that rise above the dunes and flags of the tall ships. Linger in that which we know is wordless. Still blessedly still we focus half lotus, intent on memorizing the verse. Tracing every string of the universal lattice, coy and childish for always.

We attempt. We work hard.

We mimic the thousand arms to the best of our abilities and coincidentally enough between you, me, and your grandmother, regardless of space or time our mimicry comes as a soft steady droning 'om.' Breaking barriers, tearing culture asunder. Wavering only when fragmented and hashed over the threads of varying frequencies.

But when the sun is cold, you can still find steam seeping heavily from the spaces in the door hinges of the sauna. The air inside so thick we breathe water, and the moisture knows not the difference between the surface of our eyes and the space six inches in front of them. Sound travels through granite and a trusting of my love just as soon as it ripples through the sauna steam.

So, I am singing again not because it goes unheard,

but because proven repetition ferments faith related in many
motions. I do not know where you were born or how often
and distant you travel or the means of communication you
are most comfortable traversing, so I've carved a Euro
Gothic cathedral from howlite with three crying veins of
labradorite streaking through it. The veins face three
dimensional directions so as to catch the sunlight
independently of one another so we may always see the
reflection of the universe in the things that we create,
and know which star is blazing fiercest,
just for us.

Three bells of iron rot in the three towers
emitting tones in the keys of meditation.
Whispered and cutting as sonar
finning its way through the oceans and waves.
The tails of three horse men sped relentlessly
to seek out our specific souls.
Declarations of my love
tattooed across their backs
in a triptych of organic memory.

Pieces of a whole we will each hold.

I imagine an afterlife of congruence through intention.

The three caballo we rode in on
and the horsemen that led us there.

It is in the leaving that I discover
the terraforms my heart creates.
It is in the leaving that my island
comes into sight of yours
for the very first time,
and I find coincidentally
our love, differs not that greatly.

It is no longer a struggle
to enunciate the music we play together.
For our voices will stream together as one
and emit from the core, not as a choir,
but as a single, loud, soft, steady,
'ommmmmmmmmmmmm...'

# LONGBOARDERS IN THE NIGHT

If I could bleed through the skies like I've been pressed through a fine mesh you would hear the songs I am singing to you like 174 beats per minute dancing on with no stress.

If I could race the very sun, and win and still never wear out my kicks, I know you would already be in the grass of the next morning smiling gentle eyed like the goddess you don't know you are.

But I must admit that I've been up since five and haven't napped so I don't know how far I'm going to be able to run. All the same it is so exciting that it feels like I'm going to explode with anticipation at the thought of the chase.

So, in preparation I jacked a two six of Sailor Jerry's.
Took a swig, blazed a blunt, lit a smoke and in the
soundlessness of the blaring of the countdown
just before liftoff, I see the Prime-Time crook
in the corner of your mouth.

Your eyes soften,
listening to hours of my heart pounding too fast for it's own good. But keeping a steady pace with the good of your own. All the minutes of my chest crashing compress into mere milliseconds of the sideways sly grin I reflect not knowing that all along you were the mirror.

I am beginning to ramble.

Beginning to feel dizzy and my words must be clouded and unclear, like a drunk with his gamble on account of I am so fucking high off you, it would be impossible for me to drive. So take the wheel and steer.

True, neither of us may ever come down completely. But don't worry we'll trade off every couple hours or so or on the in-betweens when we are peaking. Which needless to say at this point is probably going to be most of the time. And you know if we could we would slam the pedal to the floor and do our best to fly. Cuz fuck yea we like to go fast, and sure we like to party. But we also live in a city, so for the sake of responsibility and at least our parent's peace of mind and our own physical safety, fuck the car.

Get on your shoes.
Grab your deck.
A twenty for supplies on the way.
Your grand-dad's bag of weed
(leave a note, trust me he'll understand).
Cigars clenched between our teeth,
let out a scream,
take my hand and let's fucking go.
Let's bomb this hill
like it's the only one that exists.

Let's bomb this hill blindfolded
like we actually know what's around the bend.
Home done ink bled from our feet.
Let's ignite,
road rash
naked hips
side by side.
Long boarders
torching off
weightless,
airy, light.
Long boarders
torching off,
long, long, long,
into the night.

## HARDENED SOFTLY RITUALS

The vicious vixenish veneer
I was originally attracted to,
to my surprise, does not fade.

Even as the lazy days spiral
the crazy shades only intensify.
I touch what is touchless and find
it's grime and sheen to be real.

Even behind closed doors
her inner lime light shines.

Even laying here in the dark,
I find myself a certain clarity
and am almost childishly frantic
for the glint in her half opened
almond shaped eyes.

I pass twin mountain peaks
and cumulus clouds that open
onto blazing cool landscapes.

My stolen breath circulated.
This could be infinity.

## A FIRE'S COMA

*Passed out in the cold of your days*
*you left your last note for us to hold in our veins.*

I know people die all the time
but you were never supposed to
dwindle.
Live off of my flame.
Don't spindle into a space
where you're incapable of complaining.

You never shut off the lies before.
That's the truth of the matter
but that don't matter now.
Just speak to me, say to me anything.

Regardless of any scores we had to settle.
Any sores forlorn now not what's testing our mettle.

It's the kettle of your body
I'm certain we both feel pinned in.
But I understand I can never
fully understand the difference.
Cuz I'm feeling rotten
and you're feeling haunted,
if anything. The ghosts are battling,
crackling against the walls of your rattling breath.

Contest what's left of your best in show.
Courtesan rose fluids
flow from rows of tubes
imbuing nostrils and mouth.
Hot holes exhume from your wavered,
invaded, no longer so sacred chest.
Don't stress.
The chemicals will act as they're supposed to.

Circular but not connecting.
You strove too hard to circumvent.
Drunk on spirals I wish you could have known
how to bend to the winds of my love.
Arteries collapse when touched.
I wish you knew.
I wish you wouldn't try so hard.
If not, I might know you do.

You awaken with break neck speed.
Lucidity only means that you know you're dreaming.

Sign the deed.
Extinguish the death of flame.
In the reflection of a clockwork's face
your time remains unbeknownst,
subtly obscene and idle.
Farewells lift luck like elephants
onto one quarter inch mantles.

I am an unsettling sabre tooth unhandled.
Mammals that size cannot rest
on the weight of a one life stain.
Tell me what's the pain?
What's the song?
What went wrong?
Where's the manhole?
Dendrites of your supposed to's
fractal my presence into old dreams
where I wept into the canals of my mind's maze.

*Passed out in the cold of your days*
*you left your last note for us to hold in our veins.*

# FLIP

I'll flip my priorities as I assess the authorities.
Contemplate my moralities before I join the majorities.

Curb, womp, and blaspheme my own
for the sole sake to bend back the bone.
Watch the clean steam burn the skin.
Embrace the truth of my disfigurement
to reveal the tones. Nothing is permanent.

But I still have sewn scars
that dictate the permanence
of my exponential consistence
in the harvest of my betterment.

A lone forest I plant as a metaphor my state
as a hip-hop punk rocker in search
of a wandering home I can befriend
as my permanent residence.

No, I cannot stop wondering
what'll happen to the rest of me.
I shovel slop cuz I know it's in the dirt
that I will find the best of me.

I live as I die.
I heal as I hurt.

I am high in the sky
as I am brooding in the mirth.
Cursed, but not hexed.
Earless, but not deaf.
Taking rhyme as a token,
warmly stolen but not theft.
Bled out of quantity never of quality,
never a haughty worry and no mess.
Sightless, but still blessed.
I don't need to speak.
I don't need to stress.
I'll slaughter a thousand
to show you the creation that's left.

## JUSTICE

He hisses like miscarriages
and takes loving words like disses.
Mulled over like slumlords,
like marriages.
Like he doesn't know the difference
between backs of hands and kisses.

Less like mathematics,
more like thug's hits in the crisp darkness.
Permissive like taking lover's swords
to Teutonic submissives.
They fall to the floor in a manic steez.
Buckles and collars never electronic
but a brackish breath phonetically they breathe.
To my arrestment, not surprisingly
all things literal seem a lot like analogies lately.
Me, like barracudas and pikes.
The pope himself and the next-door dyke.
The swing and the hit.
The miss, feedback on the mic.
The drift between shutting the hell up
and screaming something that at least scares myself.
Directly under the head of my Lucky Strike.
Like reaching for the thirteen,
but only ever achieving the twelve.
Still, I hope I found what I always wanted.

My heart. The hammer.
The hieroglyphs. The level.
Like an A-bomb impacts
like morse code ripples
under mischief magma,
the hot spots I've delved.

The sulfur pools,
still, but not stagnant.
Like hotel's neon signs
full flicker but not vacant.
Like eyelids dome over
the empty spaces
where the eyes lived.
Even as the eyeless cry,
'Can I get a witness?'

Like treason.
Like the convergence of seasons
frees every man, woman, and child
can exist without grievance.
That's me, that's you, that shy cat
slinking out the back door
feeling left out, perhaps feeling alone.

But boy you should know you're never alone.
Wherever there's one introvert there's two more
just around the bend, beyond the corner.

Looking to bust out, excrete their souls,
share their sores and together we can all soar.
Hands are oars stroking the subversive.
Like the now reminds me of the when.
The has been, reminds me of the end.
Like I am of all things, and all men.
Only then, the 'like', becomes the 'is'.

And I'm learning to take the loving words
like what they are,
as love.

Ain't no disses.

Like I don't need adjectives to describe
what from love slid, what love said,
what love did,
what love meant.
Like love,
I just is.

## TWO BRIGHT STARS

Those shaking tresses of hair.
A cumulus cloud of onyx hydra spirals
like a universe surrounding the goddess
brought into illumination by the glow of your face.

The breeding novas of your eyes
pull me into the silhouette of your gravity,
and I am crushed by the weight
of the storm you personify.
By the implosion of one star into another.
The encapsulating inversion
of the invention of vision
we are manifested as.

As two vessels let go of time and space,
they will let go of the atoms between one another.
As they let go of the very earth beneath them
two bright stars explode, then vanish in a vapor.

The sound of laughter
rips through what would be called forever,
as I cannot tell where I end or where you breathe in.
In the space of two hearts synchronized palpitations,
worlds are created as lungs vocalize, and limbs begin.

## YOU CAN'T SEE ME

The jasper swelled
from where feathers sprung
to the size of gasping breaths
took upon by ghost's cellophane,
telephoning my apartment.

I swung free the door hinges
as to welcome in the poltergeists
but found myself so yellow I was orange.

Transparent as a spirit myself, a host, hazel assumed.
Neglecting the remnants reflection of fireworks
to the back side of floorboards and shelf.

 A nervous creaking sound.
A breeding ground. A mound
crafted from the wood shavings
and kindling that once were
my lookout and home.

The singes singing strings,
now only fuel for the hunger
of my ghostly brethren,
spark toothed and angling fervent.
A mistake sewn too late.
I was ripped apart by the memory of my torment.

Oh, how I cried for a chance to claim
a right to overstep the threshold
of my spaciously overpopulated inferno.
From the inside to external mount abode collapsible,
I denied the lie; intent, remappable.

I'm just the fuck out for a two-six
and a thermos of au jus we can use as chase.
Hands cupped in prayer
and drinking in the hangover.

I'll wear my soul on the outside as a warning.

I'm only visible when I let you see me.
Though the sun glares off of my ghostly teeth
in the seething palmistry that's not me and a pen breathing.
But déjà vu off your back side sneaking.
And those are the only glances you'll ever get for free.
Although you can't see me
I could let you if I was feeling just as you
could see me any way, if that's what you were needing.

Is there a poet inside me that is not a metaphor?

What becomes of my loneliness?
My solitude,
is done for.

I assume the position of a
waxed offering throat chord as it wanes.
I am thankful that understanding
my opacity is not without heart scars.

My jaw flashes and fluctuates phonetically
in and out of sight in the sunshine.
The darkness picks me out of the many planes
composing a single fluttering orb.

Waxing, waning, maybe
never beginning or ever ending.
A sigh of relief.

My solitude is done for.

# HOWL ZEPPELIN

I.

I drank you in a dream of tattooed Isis ensembles.
Stuck my seeds in obituaries denied
and I cannot be certain of the dust I've seen.
Click stacked under burden of their assemble.

I read you amidst the quiver dog's teeth.
The child inside reiterated fevers
at the touch, pastel as a surgeon's hands
detracted amongst the chemical imbalance
and tinker heavy only since you've been at my side.

Indigenous, I must remember your climate is not.
Binary, not organic but crawling backwards
as the septic woman spoke, almost mythologically so.
I cannot be one to back star any prevailed truth
surrounding legitimacy of your text feed.

The wavering transparency to your distracted eyes
of my clawing walls, is the closest your molten aircraft
to my quilled castle that you will ever come.

In a moat throat sung found torrential you are drunk.

In a wrote horns contort to tones with no dead lies,

compass is an island from which
the center of, you will find no direction.
I must remain for you
only as the foot note ascribes.
I hope for your sake,
you one night find a cedar clearing
in the out stretch of your mind.

This brass malice skirt is an island
from which the center heaves with lust.
A trench I weave to the sounds of another day.
I hoped that tomorrow I would still feel the same.

I can only hope that tomorrow I will still feel.

II.

The same dippings wet their wicks
on cuticle poems and vapor lyrics.
Flashed in a rain of passion
I cannot help but clear my throat of all this art.
I supposed at the knees of our high tides,
disengagement shone the brightest
when your radiance was nervous system electric.
A murdering experience resurrecting a woeful womb.
A joyful lamb's hoof quartered as the moon.

I fear that I will always love you.

Fear that I have been the captor
of the comfort my heart felt for falling.
I fear that I do not fear because the weight
of a birth defect's disfigurement
is a known labor of uncertainty.

Adjacent the basement and rotting bones,
a compliment for the mold's growth
knows not the edges.

Remember when the sheets
starved us of our lower halves.
We laid naked to the waist
and breathing heavily.
Enough that the sun rose
with each gaping laugh we stoked.
Loud and wide. Smiling enough
your eyes slivered the sun light
like shattered slats of shale.

Bereavement is a fiend thieving
that this is something you could ever deny.

What to do with the shearing halves
hemisphere broke the skin?
What to do to sculpt you your own
atmosphere on this crowded planet?
What to do to stitch the fault lines back together?

What was less, was you had what was more.
What was more was that I spat physics as consistently
as your quantum philosophy built a crack we could touch.

How the two between could ever let us in?

III.

Howling zeppelins scarring underbellies.
Texture reminiscent of mountain tops rubbed smooth.
The fires still ember strongly, naturally.

I find a new summit opposite the plateau
for us to create worlds still.
Simply under a sunset glinting aurora
in a tremulant of fresher hues.
Fractal jazz,
the flora and fauna.

What happens in the holding bay of a cliff ward zeppelin
when there are no formations for it's descent
besides the painting aft chain from the sky?

You just let it hit the water.

# GRIMOIRE

Stoned and pressed together
under the over cast sky,
I couldn't tell if the heart beat
I was feeling was yours or mine.

Inside the air and soft rocks mossy manuscript
of moisture upheld the manipulation
of our contour capsized looking glass.

Your dark eyes narrow, peering
through the emptiness of mine
like well buckets with no bottoms.
Seeing only coins of silver lost in
the mud of some other spinning forest.

Coniferous tree bodies glistening glossy
and dripping with the previous night's rain.

When the petrichor hits,
the momentum of our monument
is reduced to a mere moment.

One sneaker on the moon,
an ounce of wane,
then it's back on the asphalt.
Alone once again.

# FORGIVE

The vocoder,
the ambient strings
and transient pads
remind me of
desolate landscapes,
clutching a melancholy
capable only in the winds
and exhaust of my dreams.

Cities left

shadowed.

No one
will ever see.

This time

I cannot forgive.

## I ONLY WANT TO LIVE

Give me honor and respect, and
strength and hope and active potential,
and solace and integrity and trust and
honesty and belief in my fellow man.

Give me community and laughter.
Give me unconditional passion.
Give me forgiveness,
the capacity for a deeper hunger
and the capacity to forgive.

Give me a genuine understanding of myself
as an individual, myself as a direct influence,
and myself as a collective soul.

Give me a place in the dirt.

Give me sanctuary,
a jaw versed enough
to defend with words spoken,
and bones blinding destruction
upon the hate of my enemies
and skulls broken.
But most of all,
give me truth and love,
and a humble head amongst it all.

BLUE

The cigarette filter is rough
and cuts my lip as I drag,
pull away and cough.

The stinging spot of blood
offers me a glimpse,
a hint,
towards birthday ribbons.

Wishes pulled from my mouth
stifled by the smoke, and my last
honest glint attempt at finally,
saying something beautiful.

# THE REED'S NOTE

I've got clothes that I own
and I wear them fine in water color
and the shine of dawn
cutting a heavy stitch across my trousers,
lowers my brow and hand full of flowers
until they are level with the eye
and Glock embedded waist line.

Style bred of a violet horizon and violence
that only I have been the shark to witness.

I recognize zen then, as a pad of sound.
Second nature thirsty for the drink
as a grape vine is for the nurturing.

Could I bereave the closing iris of day
across ego's chimera and be led away to
wherever it is that I will find myself tomorrow?

The sun dodger's cleft chin split the stars
and the reflection of the moon light
off the sea's spite off my two eyes
are the only halves that are left.

Fingering the crevices between clouds.
The past we lost track of.

Only once found could we have been
open enough to have been right here,
right now, shortly in the future.
While behind us the hidden hues
of the purples and oranges
and green rusted door hinges.
We followed by sight alone
since choices I suppose find me
with zero decibels worth of scent.
But in the modest hints of light
faint shadows glissando off the might
of the teeth in my now extra mouth.

That is the momentum of the note of the reed.
A peace is the permanence, a predicate of the seed.

The sun is always setting and spills
like O.E. on the concrete.

The wolves and sleep meet
where poltergeists digest rhythm.
The apex of the sky, my one holy moment.
Palms pressing between solar systems,
infinity has frozen.

## AS I REACH MY REPLY

So what else is there?
I'm spinning a good yarn
and so far,
the tapestry's coming along.
I'm singing that bright song
and yet, it ain't got no words.

Still I hope you heard everything I said.
From way over by the crash of the curb
to the slashing of the mosh and
the ever-loving heat of the pit.
To every comfort you found in bed.
Every sound in every phone,
in every tone, in every head.
The message, it remains the same.
Always in it's truest colors
never smothered or too bled.

The conflicts for the most part they don't stick.
They wash away while their residue sustains
the positivity like silence and chemistry, a new mix.
Softened hues like my sober intoxicated new view.
I found a new drink that offers proper cause
to my new bruised and closed eye moves.
Some pass it off as a case of public drunkenness.

But if love is illicit then I think
I'm just the bandit you've been looking for.

If it is unlawful to be high as a mother fucker
off the wordless passion I have for every brother,
sun shine and moon light and all of creation;
then I will gladly don the chains and steel collar
that the fearful have fashioned,
and I will wear them until the last rising dawn.
Shake my split end tresses in time
with the last note of the last song.
The last words spoke,
they carry on.

Desolate but not famished.
My love remains
but the body has vanished.
The chains clamber
to the ground, silent.
My body is not just external.
My passion, eternal.
As I reach my reply,
my love is a fractal.

# AURORA

Time and space
Form the X & Y Axis
oF valleys and RidgeS.
oF our Location
nobody asks us.

My hand into pen to ink turns the paper
before / & right wrong / but not after
of that which feeds us
soul and laughter
our faces in the fire / glow /
go to where our mountains are eyelids
looking out
with no grimacing cringes.

## DAFFODIL

You can't fast forward
through music
whose intention it is,
is to bring attention
to it's progression.

Life is beautiful.

## PIRATES

Gut wrenching tear the roof off set the house on fire
scream spit and blaspheme bloody murder into the speakers
screaming back louder than you ever could sweat of my
sweat blood of my blood from the windows to the walls every
day and every night for all that is holy and all that is right
unabashedly vulnerable brooding violent ineffable creating
everything just to destroy it and build it back as something
even more effortless weightless sightless undaunted
deranged always sustained and all ways relentless,

love.

## A WHISKING EXISTENCE

A dreaming earth harbors no expectancy.
Meteor showers collide with deep oceans.
Volcanoes speak loudly in time and
cadence with one another to the
rise and fall of the birth of new islands.
Changing with no will in their subtleties
the tides rise as the sea's surface area decreases.

Nothing is created and nothing is destroyed.

An endless wash of change,
and still the earth dreams on.
Never questioning.
Pure awareness.
Pure sensation.
A dreaming world, simply breathes on.

# REPLENISH

My bass stance streams symbiotic
like the mind interprets sounds
in movement akin to phonetics.

All around the world
our vocab remains vernacular.

Manifesting monoliths
with every dub breath.
Flame thrower steps
like I'm fire on the inside,
oxygenated on the regular.

Grin wide, grim wise.
I got the grimoire
packed with good intention.
Convex direction
until it's something sly and cyclical.
A thousand circling spells of suspension
to mislead the grime lies into new times.
They move in many ways.
My mind strays like any and
everything plays every day.
Man, I wish I could stay but
when I lay my body pulls me
in every way but linear.

My steps in trance,
the cleft clef leaves me deaf.
If you bleed me fresh,
I'll blend right into the mess.
Never to be missed,
cuz in death I never left
my prospective just shifts.
My vision only lifts.
My provision never
sits too still, for too long.
Singing that same song.
Repetition along with faith
it can only ferment.
So, I spit it one more time
yes, I spit it again.

My purity is eternal,
perpetually replenished.
Coalescence in the afterglow.
After death I'm never finished.
Flowing on tomorrow,
the whispering winds say I'm blessed.
Their current gives me strength,
gives me solace, gives me rest.
The earth gives me direction,
my quests I don't question.
I touch the dirt, I taste the water,

the humility of my direction.
Trusting the melody.
The sustenance I deserve.
Of myself I give freely,
so I know I'll never thirst.
I am the wetlands where
every morning I am birthed.
I may wake sleepy
and with bed head
but still I move freely.
When I strike a pose,
it's with laughter.
When I strike a verse,
it's with method.
When I close my eyes,
I listen keenly.
Find my root and my base,
from the ground to the rafters.
In the light of day
I do not hesitate to pray
for the gods are all around me.
We talk all the time.
I am here for the dance.
For the rhythm.
For the rhyme.

## PAGAN

Sistine cobras
deleted from the ceiling.

In the future they'll believe
man used to live in the sky.

We've now severed ourselves from the poison,

the healing and all that.

The worn bellies of roads we've rode
have hidden the scales from our eyelids,
and the antlers from our ears.

To hide our paws from the dirt
they will fan out their hoods,
bare their fangs,

and ignore the rest of our body.

## STANDING GROUND

I be faint like a crook
with his gimmick written over.
Looking over shoulder,
barely missed the boulder.
Lucky like a clover.
Through the gate before it's closure.
I extinguish hate with the moan of pleasure.
My hormonal leisure is never lackadaisy
but damn that shit is heavy.

If you're curious you don't have to wait
cuz I already got five fingers under your belt.
They're furious as fuck and bound to bust the levy.
I'm crawling through the cracks and please believe
that ain't water that fills the spaces.

I pry open my rhyme book and between the pages
I got 88 keys that lay in wait, still and breathing
as a woman's lace. I pluck with my pen
and amplify with my tongue.
With these two hands is how I bring the bass.
With the purple glow of my instrument,
that's how this song is sung.

Black and white and all the tones in between.
From fuck until fight from dark into light

from strike into struck I play your tune perfectly.
I do not recognize the color, but the sound is so familiar.
So if these vibrations lend your ear, then splendid.
We'll let one another be the paths upon which we slither,
suspended. As we dance back and forth
the flame of the torch only rising higher.
The trance and perfection.
The beauty, how at its mere suggestion
I see before me only progression.
Direction's in the back seat but he is still driving.
There are always deadlines to meet,
so I make malleable my space and my time
cuz I believe that I can make
any and everything into anything I want
simply with the power of my will
and the machine of my mind.

I be faint like a crook with his gimmick written over.
I be slight as the shadows that I'm ripping through.
Looking over shoulder, barely missed the boulder.
Lucky like a clover, yea that's how I fucking do.

# PLAGUE APRON

Pinching pennies
like microscopic
syringes and lances.

Free.99 face lifts,
hot Aston Martins
and lass's asses.

I bottle the passing of gases
like they're sacramental omens
for the futures of masses.

# 12 FOOT SPEAKER SPOKE THE LION NOW WATCH ME FLOAT

The backs of my hands
peel into palms
and another gripping ten.
The nails they grow
to a march sounding
of bone and flow.
A heave exponential and a
fractaling of my instrument.

About a centerless river
where no dividing crux
or knuckle bend
can tear or defend,
I find a jointful temple.
Rich with current
I am finally capable of balancing
without attempting to grip.

I am a body of soft palms.
No clutch,
though far from fingerless.
I just breathe,

and let the bliss rest.

## TOP HAT

Satisfied by the sax,
rafters collapse.
Lavish snacks.
Laps that snap.
Paths tattooed like this
one-man army tracks his prey.
Engage the zombies.
Crack open the bodies
and let whatever come that may.

Apocalyptic present intrinsically.
I seethe with a rotten, bawdy attitude.
Slot spattered gilded headpiece
wheezed distressingly in a different light.
This time she burns vertically
across them lines of latitude.
Gratitude reigns as servitude.
Slain to circumvent not mine,
but our better view.
Vanquished bitter vantage point,
advantage to the prior skewed.

A driven engine and catalyst
as I'm made of all kinds of shit.
Infinite percentages
like all the world's cures

can't hack my prime directive.

This maker spoke the seed of life into being planted.

This master choked on the atom
to bring forth Eve and her Adam.
Now imagine what will happen
when I put intention behind this spit.
Aim the barrel at the temple of myself
and the universe and let that shit go,
'click.'

# RONIN

I jet some good grace from out my window sill, fairly.

The passing of time vanquishes into scarcity.

The poplars settle just right in amongst the foxglove.

As she emerges from the hot springs,
the snow still falls,
slowly.

Mountain peaks cry between the cloud's fat hunger.
I am reminded of her love
as she merges with the nature around her.
My sight remains sharp but her tears tear my blade asunder.

The distance is killing me.
As it lessens the lessons fully render
the questions quest for sustenance
and we feed together, tender.

Tying together moments in smoke,
the venison ages into leather.
The protection and battle-ready armor
will sound so loudly under this very same sky.
Violence and silence feather to the body.
Tethered to the undercurrents

only time surrenders, shoddy.
Blether our words like worms
into the homes of our mutual enemies.
Tie the veins off to allow
survival in light of the severing.
Slight our eyes and let our
intertwined hands do the teething.

Together we feast
on the fertile soil of spilt sacred space.
We toil and leave nothing but the ash of our war.
The gore that god left in the wake of our breath's
moisturizing trace transforms manmade lakes
into something our wings ought to get a hold of.

As she and I fold together
perfect symmetry becomes natural.

Branches fall to the forest floor.

The clouds no longer hunger.
She and I kiss, peace, love, give thanks
as we shed the skins of our tanks and finally sublimate.

## WHALE BONES

Wrenches clatter downwards
through the cloud of pots and cast-iron pans.

Inside the joints of all tools
the only constant consists of concepts.

Even consciousness
eventually collapses,
enveloping continuity.

Eventually cooking,
becomes baking,
becomes burnt.

A twist of a purse,
the bent knee of a skirt,
and still amongst the flash fire,
the gas and the char;
still something,
must be presented.

Calamity, they once called me.
They are on this day, nobody.
So at the moment I go by nothing.

You've your legs crossed

and the table cloth helps not with hiding.

I can tell by the way you bite your lip
when I set this plate in front of you
and also, by the way you're slouching.

They used to call you Vicky.
Only so that when they did you'd
know how little they cared as to
what name you had actually been given.

I figure I touched a nerve
as you looked away.
Pouring towards the ceiling
like it was the top of your foot,
the back of your knee.
Your hip, your palm.
Your face.

You take a bite.
The steam wafts through you porously and
I've been on the subject of you for so long
by fork down both shoes removed
I'm rubbing the spaces between your toes.
You grin, and already know too much.

As I shut my mouth,
the table vanishes.

The chairs standoffish.
The consonance of our touch.
Our bodies conduct rhythm.
The rhyme between us belonging
to the assonance of our past.

Alliteration is not a topic of which we spoke
unless in hushed onomatopoeia
we cut from each other's shade,
we gut from each other's tone.
Everything we've ever been reinvented
by one another with instinct so honest
your shame and secret become me.

My vulnerability leaves you writhing
and in the hot box of the kitchen floor.

We playfully pressed blades
against each other's throats

waiting for our lips to part,
and for one of us to breathe.

# PERENNIAL

This young chrysanthemum
crisp as a chrysalis,
frozen in the tip
of a wet dripping icicle.

Her static silence crackling outwards.
Vibrating growth within the emptiness.

Blossom has come to change.

We leave this time, leafless.

Paw prints in the white out percolate in the cold.

Our breath levitates,
permanent.

A cricket's lisp
will always go unnoticed.

## RUNNING FROM REAPER

I think I smoke too much.
I stumble and fumble around
and spit up my gut like lunch.
Fidget fucked and crutched.
Rinse washed and crunched.

From OshKosh B'gosh to modern day slop I'm not sure that I've lost anything at all. I still got the bat of my spine and the ball of my skull, but do I got a reason to be grumbling around with a hole in my soul? Do I got a hold of the whole? Nada. Low note blown by blotter. Stolen remote trigger. Barrel pointed right at you. Melee attack from this righteous rottweiler. No real weapons, but heavy paws and god handlers. Swinging piñatas in front of sightless Jehovahs in the inner depths of the projects during winter it was home was blown by snow to cut zones by lines of blood proper. Fruit of my loins dictate not a thing. Since family not so familia in the deuce eye patched sting of these po' cop caught called redeemer.

Here comes a freight fraught with my insecurities. Fought off in a single shot. Hennessey heisted heresy hips and cheeks gaunt. Mother Mary massacred barely under a cloud of mustard gas, now a fetishy gas mask she dons. A million buildings domino 'til the walls gone.

The horizon's sun sung songs lost to the slung and ruthless only when my guardian angel ain't present. I wake up in a pool of black gesso paint and apex the windows blown inward away from tresses.

I'm not seventeen no more,
so I don't wear dresses.
I'm not twenty-one no more,
so I don't clean up drunk girl's messes.
I'm not twenty-five on the dot no more neither,
so I don't linger on lessons.
I cop the betterment like every second
I'm the better man's mettle.
Lyrics melt into metal
to become grooves in the vinyl.
Hot wax inside the presses.

I make a lot of sound but I'm still running from reaper. I make puddles in the ground, but can't put a face to the deceiver. Can't put a trace on the receiver. Can't get an opinion from any of my selves or any minion, so I figure my phone must be off the hook. And I'm shook baby, tell me what's my choice. I got the reaper outside and the cleaver within. Balance is a tricky bitch but I fuck tight ropes with a shadowed brow and a shiny grin.

This ain't no stint.
This is lifelong, and I don't mean until I kick it.

I mean from never and on forever. Tears from a meteor tore
the atmosphere a new few thousand potential flight
believers, now we're scrying the next evolution in Moon and
Mars dust. How soon until the aliens pour out my wounds to
pry my third eye into opening up? Tears from a samurai
never touch the dirt. So I'm learning how to be a cloud
jumper from those warriors who got nothing
but their own to quench their thirst.

And I'm learning.
Yea I'm learning about code and about honor.
Not a word, I am the thread and I am the pin. I am the strike
of the bullet and spear, precipitation inside the sauna
keeping speech to a min. Shipwrecks found in the top halves
of mountains and they said I was absurd. I am a seamless
face, bounty saturated 'til blurred. A killer with two sharp
fingers in a bucket of paint. Carve out the negative space.
Black gesso drench the vase. Dress disintegrates to lace so I
don't have to guess her layers. So deco or fresco, whatever
have you in the back seat soliloquy spun from the land mine
of my heart. Heaven only once the windows opaque with
your skin. But you're no vehicle so I don't, just, can't, not
gonna give a damn. Cuz I got the reaper outside and the
cleaver within. Balance is a tricky bitch but I fuck tight ropes
with a shadowed brow and a shiny grin.

## GREEN TEA AND WEED SMOKE

Green light spilling past the peeling paint
on the slanted wooden window frame
fills the claw foot tub.

Cracked porcelain.

Inside, astro freckles, flicker.
Constellations spanning your length
and blinking in the steam and mist of your magic.

In the living room I roll a blunt
proper for a queen like you.

By the moonlight,
the splash of bath water
sounds so pure, just knowing
it is a sound you made.

Tonight, the TV sleeps.

## UNDERWATER SONGS TO DIE TO

I stink like deer meat,
coffee, cigarettes
and blueberry juice.

The trampling caused the paths
upon which we pause now.

My needing, no longer wanting.
My phalanx tooth shimmies through.

Lose the noose.
Loose fresh
goose neck bled.
The tongue's proof,
we laid to bed.

What a grave the sound of pianos has become.
What a widow.

Her death gave way
to these weighing waves.
Gaze I raise from palms that pray.
Psalms of silence,
hymns hinge on haze.
Hands slack behind my back
as I grip the splitting cells.

Blindfold held 'til I turn away.

Only time would tell.
But my love, my belle,
do you remember?
We collapsed the skull
under water in light of the swell.

We cut out the heart
to cease the smell.

Senses fuckered.
Directions rudder.
The base got harder
as the fins fade darker.
We touch the bottom
to rise again.

Death by pressure.

My aquatic bones begin to bubble.

## MAY YOUR TEA NEVER GO COLD

Don't let the frantic
dawn bloodshed in the rat pit.
Open up the comatose.
Shed light onto the vanished.
Breathe air into the lungless.
Break the speed of sound
with bass blown from the lamp lit.
Trace clones. Now throw,
eliminating the duplicates.

Shadowed faces
dropped down and out.
Blade, feign to pout.
Freight sought to catch.
Rip wide the batch.
Slay wash the match.
Smoke 'em if you got 'em
cuz I flail like I'm haunted.
Burn dreams like braille
like I'm too frail,
still out for the wanted.
All static, no stale.
Wind to the sails
like I haven't forgotten
that the spirit won't last.
The dotted line's been predetermined.

Cut and paste and all senses slashed
but we are still of the vermin.
So bottoms up humans of humans
and drink deep.

Cuz I'm still here yo.
'Til the last daft, the last crash,
the last laugh, the last sermon.
Ya steeped.
Knuckles to knuckles,
heart of the secrets we keep.

# THE YARD

Raiding your parking lot
like panty hose got holes.

Clouding centrifugal sensory forces
to meet and maim the darkened ocelot.

The past enfolds
like gold jewels adorn the nose.

A Rasta ruse.
A crime between me and you.

A riot.

A matchstick born of ballerina orca stitch pirouette.

An orchestra slung,
drunk,
heavy in the wings.

We can get this bird to fly,

it just ain't done being built yet.

## SAFFRON

I'm de-looping the hard 3 street block rooster
to let him reroute the coup mischief.
Phoenix freed from out the soup mixture.
Now her fury's gone stock
to the pots gone drip, drip, drip.

Splat out the ceiling fixtures.
Now this slurry comes coupled
with rough floor splinters.
Saving the tips of my fingers
for eating out the sugar cane dinner.
When I'll be groovy sly whiskers,
that tongue's got my cat
'til the barstool's 6 foot five.

I don't know how to measure
but that's some percentage of meters.
As long as vintage replaces the fowl,
suffering succotash will have me
less concerned about how,
the feathers got in than I am
about how to get them out.

You put away the latches
and went straight for the comb.

Crowing heavy through the wires of your old downtown.
You flew until your claws water colored behind you.
Blending your DVS kicks into the manhole gradient.

And baby,
you got spray paint on your eyelashes
and whimsy in your lips.
I forgot that last rhyme entirely
when I saw you on the strip.
Inky mushroom finger prints are all to me you gift.
The crystals ran away and still you linger like a lisp.
My rhythm reaches and sways to carve out across your hips
and find the playing strings of where two instruments exist.

I been plucking these hairs 'til my beard bleed thin.
Thinking on how to meow that little door swing.
She sneers perpendicular to my parallel grain,
but we both know the truth like that ain't her name.
Calling here pussy, pussy. Here, pussy puss.
Still rambling on like different is the same,
like the gut's still pink, what a lie to the brain.
Like the rudder sun sunk under weight of the strain.
So, the bow moon rose just to light a new day.

You flew 'til your claws watercolored behind you.
Bending your DVS kicks into the manhole gradient.

## OMNITEMPO MAXIMALISM

If it seems that I've keeping my speech to a minimum.
It's not that I'm not speaking.
It's the position from where the words are leaking.
Just another dendrite adding harmony to the flow.
From laughter to where the silence runs.
Om mani padme hum.
I ain't ever started and I ain't ever done
and I ain't got to speak to be heard
or be anyone special to be the cure
or make the line to know it curves.
Cuz in the past I've been destruction,
been creation and in between
I find my balance preordained.
I'm deep enough to know myself,
to take the gun out of my chest,
replace it with my heart.
Stash the death up on the shelf.
Life knows what's best, participate
and be a part and say what you have to say.
Cuz in the flow it all just glows,
it all just goes to show.
It ain't what you know,
it's what you're learning
that keeps the world turning.
Word. Word.
Let's keep this fire burning.

## AND ON / NOD

This front-end gut and same old shit.
I dizzy down and guzzle up.
Smut abrupt, bubble cut,
I find the right and like to pick.
Locks are scabs that trick my wit.
Mask the process of healing
underneath the blemished skin.
Stronger doors that once before,
comfort then, now vanquishment.
Golden wraiths that I adorn.
Stolen praise I can't afford.
Polarity strays on sullen sores
and under ancient rays
a sacrifice is made.
A promise to entice.
The effort made was more
but somehow less than what
was originally appraised.
Do we ever really need to know
what we've bargained for?
What we killed and what we made,
I cannot tell the difference any more.

# NOD / AND ON

You've all been tricky
since I've been on that glass.
Staring heavy, light like fast.
Flex note steady, bass done blast.
Spot light shone. Smoke not gone.
Puff, puff, pass, we're never wrong.
We played that song and never asked.
No apologies.
Here the narc's done dead, the skid's been fed.
The spark's after glow once a purple, now is red.
As gravity moves the tide,
these pulsing waves can only grow.
I no longer believe in time.
But I believe in time
that I will come to know.

# BOTTLED GODS

Guns that twitch make the blitz squid crash.
Rush the whole crowd,
make their trigger fingers do the slashing.

Do the slush thing 'til the sun ring.
Dude, do what you want to cuz I'm on you
like the Antarctic snow mobile dash dew.

Trash grew, and as we tried to,
a few flew the coup out the man hole.
Grazer's gaze drawn long to the sky
where pop a soul to hold a clue,
but the herd got nada.

Slaughter sound to sight.
Laughter, ladder, lighter
cattle grew horns to fight.
Ratchet between Wichita
and here man, I'm born to bite
the wick of the candle
when the witch stack burns too bright.
Take the slick off the mantle
and the paint off the white walls.
This bed of broken windows,
willows and widows, they hold too tight.

So I'll gobble the throttle,
wobble like a rainbow,
blow out the fourth floor
like molotov's and gods
built inside of bottles.

What is your cocktail?
Whatever your poison
I'll smash everything in the cellar
and let the gods drink together.
I will drink of the gods
as the gods drink of me.
Let the noise pour in,
let the seasons go free.

# HEAD TILT EARTH CUBE

I'm all the puff what with my anterior helix.
I look like a chipmunk from one angle only.
2D platformer. My other half thin and lonely.
A half breed between Alvin and Felix.

The techno of today,
and the third eye of the Arctic Sphinx.
The penguins shy away
while the narwhale's always up for a boning.

The pyramids spun into coning,
Earth would look like a cube
if it ever stopped rotating.

## STILL MY SKULL'S SHADOW

Through remembering the shadows
and minding my matter
I have become capable of self-sublimation.

I have been there since before the coming of before,
and returned to the present to tell of the after.
To tell of the self that we lay to let fire.
Desecration upon the altar.
The mandala that fell
as human hands reached out
through the skulls and the tears
and pried open the laughter.
Released the light that broke,
whoa, there go the rafters.
The sunshine, balance like change,
now presses as heavy as disaster.

Nothing stays the same.
All love and all pain, always lost, always gained.
I reside in the womb every time that I dream
and I'm of new birth every time that I wake.

On a mountain all our own, we rise above.
We identify, engage, exhume, confide,
confront and eliminate all that is inside.
Unhindered we find freedom from ourselves.

So now let us give of ourselves.
Let us dash away the knives,
keep the gun up on the shelf.
Tear off our armor
and let all that hurt melt.
Touch that vulnerable murmur
and when the pulse keeps pace,
we'll let that waltz be the face.
Let the room spin,
just let the vision shake.

## DARK JADE TORTOISE

I'm a tinder tiny cabin
raving little splinter,
flashing fire never tire
twisted spire of a miser.

Geysers sputter sulphur.
Simple home, the master's back.
Supple dome in subtle chrome
I must have heard the whale phone.
I dread the sea in all it's tones
my breath it's held 'til I react.

The woods they open up to me.
Cleavage heat and steamy seed.
Bend the moss to meet my knees
and hear the stones go crack.

Heed the error, tactical.
My bayonet gone radical.
Slay a jet and what do you get?
A six-barrel hooker from Saigon.
A billion people screw loose
from one day to the next.

Let bygones be bygones,
so we can go and get the hell on.

Trace the alley ways and cans of paint.
This saint he smells of Krylon.

A decent dude injects a silo
as I down my glass of vino.

The wings begin to dip,
flying low my cobra vow.
We're going down,
oh, what's that sound
this shape like cloud
and could I fit?

I mold like spit and razor burns.
Breaking bread with broken bones.
Crushing wine with scars I've earned.
Opening up and letting go.

A riot feast.
A place we know,
ransacked violently.
I do not understand,
but I hear
the voicing fear
of my pious greed;
the humble god
I need to grow.

A liquid state.
A colic quake
my inner lake,
resuscitate.

Here's to one last ship.
One more sip.
One last drip of O.E.
on the concrete
for the deceased,
finally starting to get a grip.
Learning to rock a crease.
To shut my mouth
and please believe;
that dark jade tortoise,
damn right I be.

Large soft steps
sunk wide and deep.
The beat goes on,
and on with thee.

The beat goes on,
and on with thee.

www.ingramcontent.com/pod-product-compliance
Lightning Source LLC
Chambersburg PA
CBHW050244120526
44590CB00016B/2204